# New Life

Cherie Werner

The mission of CTA is

to glorify God by providing purposeful products
that lift up and encourage the body of Christ!

because we love him.

Copyright © 2008 CTA, Inc., 1625 Larkin Williams Rd., Fenton, MO 63026-1205
www.CTAinc.com

Scripture taken from the HOLY BIBLE, NEW INTERNATIONAL VERSION®. Copyright © 1973, 1978, 1984 International Bible Society. Used by permission of Zondervan. All rights reserved.

ISBN 978-1-933234-54-0
Printed in Thailand.

I am a caterpillar.
I hardly make a sound.

I look for lots of leaves to eat up high

and on the
ground.

And as I eat,
my body grows.
I'm ready for
a change.

I wrap up in
a chrysalis;
it looks so
very strange.

Though it may seem
to those who watch
that inside I could die,
our God is making
something new—

See, now,
a **butterfly!**

# A Note to Grown-Ups

"In the beginning God created the heavens and the earth. . . . God saw all that he had made, and it was very good" (Genesis 1:1, 31).

Because of God's great love for us, he surrounds us with the incredible beauty of creation. In creation he shows us many different examples of the way he works in our lives. We experience the beauty of new life, growth, maturity, death, and rebirth. We see this in the cycle of the seasons, as we watch seeds grow into flowers, and as caterpillars become butterflies.

In this same way God works in each one of us as he calls us to faith in Jesus and transforms our hearts and lives with his Spirit.

If possible, take your child outside to read this book. After reading the book, take some time to sit and enjoy the wonder of God's creation. Look. Listen. Smell. Touch. Talk about what you experience together. Talk about how God can take something old and make it new.

Celebrate God's gift of new life with your child and praise God for his great love! "How great is the love the Father has lavished on us, that we should be called children of God! And that is what we are!" (1 John 3:1).

~ Cherie Werner